LITTLE THINGS

A DEVOTIONAL

Michael Petway Jr.
Cover art by: W. DeQuentin Dickey

ISBN 979-8-89130-657-8 (paperback)
ISBN 979-8-89130-658-5 (digital)

Christian Faith Publishing
832 Park Avenue
Meadville, PA 16335
www.christianfaithpublishing.com

All Bible verses are from the Christian Standard Bible unless annotated otherwise.

Printed in the United States of America

To my bride, I love you

To my daughters, I cherish you

To my parents and foundation, I appreciate you

*To every person who has walked with me
during this journey, I thank you*

Although this work was a labor of love, we highly encourage your engagement with this devotional to be simply a starting point of your interaction with the Bible and your local church.

We would appreciate hearing how this book has impacted you and prompted you to dive deeper into a relationship with Jesus. Please email us at TheLittleThingsDevo@gmail.com.

Contents

Introduction

This book serves as a reminder that with humanity's grand chasms and big differences, hope and perspective can still be garnered in the contemplation of life's little things.

Little Issue, Big Problem

In 1912, the maritime vessel dubbed *Titanic* prepared to make her maiden voyage. British naval officer David Blair had the menial task of keeping the keys that opened a cabinet containing the crow's nest binoculars. He was abruptly reassigned to another ocean liner just days before the first expedition. However, in his haste to gather his belongings, he failed to turn over the keys to his relief. Subsequently, the cabinet that held the crow's nest binoculars remained locked.

This would be a meaningless footnote in the *Titanic*'s narrative if the steamship did not meet its fate of doom by an iceberg collision. Consequently, it was not an iceberg initially that caused the sinking of the *Titanic*. Instead, it was the slight issue of missing keys that resulted in a big problem. Similarly, the roots of our emotional history can expose themselves in extreme ways if gone unresolved. Minor issues can also become big problems.

As icebergs are deceptively large, so, too, are the effects of one's words. The story of the *Titanic*'s locked binoculars illuminates the importance of examining ourselves to ensure our part in our pain is minimal. In James, the author speaks of the correlation between spiritual and emotional maturity. James 1:26 warns, "If anyone thinks he is religious without controlling his tongue [words], his religion is useless, and he deceives himself."

The principle is to not be ruled by emotions. This practice ignites the process of emotional maturation and, thusly, reveals where we are spiritually.

Little thought: Adversity reveals what's under the surface.

What could be resolved if you seek the keys to emotional and spiritual maturity?

Happy Hour at the Well

Happy-hour festivities consist of several mainstays that include entertainment and social interaction, but primarily, these times include drinks at a discounted price. One of the first recorded instances of this can be found in Exodus 2:11–22. This passage shows a man running from his past and resting at a water well. This man, named Moses, had youthful ambition without mature discernment, which drove him to kill a man in an episode of rage. In line with most emotionally driven decisions, he was confronted about his lapse in judgment and left town as quickly as he could. He ran from his trouble, only to find that trouble was not only chasing but also within him.

He encountered seven sisters who were being mistreated at the well and aggressively settled the dispute on their behalf. He not only saved the day but also retrieved water from the well for them. Moses possessed leadership qualities but needed at least forty years of refinement. Verse 18 shows their

4

father's inquiry about why the trip to fill the water jugs was so short. They told their father that they were able to acquire and enjoy the well water for a bargain thanks to a foreign man.

Moses delivered these women from desert thugs and, later, a nation from the clutches of an unjust ruler. With time, Old Testament prophets would announce a future deliverer for all people. Consequently, we find ourselves back at a well. In John 4, a woman and a foreign man sat at a well and talked. This man, named Jesus, had youthful ambition and a maturity that loved indiscriminately. She spoke of the physical water that could satisfy her thirsty throat, but Jesus spoke of a water that would quench her thirsty soul. This woman at the well with Jesus—and the women with Moses—simply had to do what humanity has been offered to do, which is to accept what has been paid for and enjoy the free refills.

> Blessed are those who hunger
> and thirst for righteousness, for
> they will be filled. (Matthew 5:6)

Little thought: If life had a grand dispenser, what could you use a refill of?

Hide-and-Seek

For any parent or those who reflect on fleeting youth, one truth emerges: time flies. No matter the age or the background, one thing seldom changes: children love games. One game that maintains popularity is hide-and-seek. As a child hides in a closet, you can hear their giggles from miles away. As they snicker behind a curtain, they feel they've found the world's best hiding place, not realizing their bodies are covered but their feet are in clear view.

Such behavior is far removed from adults, right? As adults, we sometime hide from hard conversations, responsibilities, and many other things. Avoidance, for most, comes naturally because it feels comfortable. However, God has not hidden Himself or His intent from humanity. Contrarily, humanity naturally leans away from God. I can only imagine the galactic-sized smile God must get out of us trying to hide our faults when we are very visible to Him. Isaiah 55:6–7 shows this: "Seek the Lord while he may be found; call to him while he is near. Let the wicked one abandon his way and the sinful one his thoughts; let him return to the Lord, so he may have compassion on him, and to our God, for he will freely forgive."

Little thought: There is no need to hide anything. He knows all our secrets yet loves us passionately.

The Hard Work of Rest

Teaching children can be defined as the hard work of repetition until learning takes place. One such lesson is that of the consequences of lying. Little humans mirror big humans in working hard to evade trouble. They assess the situation and state partial facts to escape the consequence of punishment. In some instances, you see a child commit an act, and the child will still deflect, deny, and counter-accuse.

Although as children and adults we have lied, God has not and cannot lie. This introduces an interesting paradox. Psalm 121:4 says, "God does not slumber or sleep." But in Genesis 2:3, after He created all things, on the seventh day he rested. How do we interpret these seemingly contradictory statements? Has God lied?

God is not a human who needs rest; however, in Genesis He was establishing a prescribed way of life, which is a rhythm of rest. This was more clearly established in the Ten Commandments, in Exodus 20:8: "Remember the Sabbath and keep it Holy."

The heart of this principle is not a literal six consecutive days of work, then rest, nor was it meant to be a millennia-old debate on the Sabbath being a Saturday or Sunday. Ultimately, the big idea is to engrain a healthy rhythm that not only rests the body but also reminds the heart of its true provider.

Little thought: Resist the never-ending pursuit of doing and embrace the hard work of rest.

Open-Door Policy

An open-door policy is often established in professional and educational settings. This gesture is when an employer or educator stresses the freedom of access and encourages the frequency of visits. Psalm 141:3 petitions, "LORD, set up a guard for my mouth; keep watch at the door of my lips." When it comes to the *doors of our lips*, we regularly embrace an open-door policy when we choose not to exhibit a filter between what we think and the words we speak. Many are even convinced that their life's calling is to, constantly, offer unsolicited advice. James 1:26 admonishes, "If anyone thinks he is religious without controlling his tongue [words], his religion is useless, and he deceives himself."

As our words seek to fly free, we must petition God to take control and learn to sometimes close our "doors"!

Little thought: The pink tornado of our tongue can impact the trajectory of many lives.

See, Salivate, Suffer

There is a familiar story credited to the renowned Greek storyteller Aesop about a relatable dog. Aesop's fable speaks of a butcher who was closing his shop for the day and chose to throw a neighborhood dog a bone. This dog was running home with his prize at top speed and approached a narrow footbridge. He happened to look down and saw another dog in the mirrored image of the water. The greedy dog began to salivate for the bigger bone; and instead of thinking, he dropped his bone and pounced toward the image in the river, only to find himself swimming frantically to reach the shore.

Like the dog, our human nature is to want what we do not have, and we are often compelled to cross any bridge to satisfy that appetite. The origin story of humanity's innate desire for more can be found in the beginning.

Genesis 3:6 records, "The woman saw that the tree was good for food and delightful to look at, and that it was desirable for obtaining wisdom. So, she took some of its fruit and ate it; she also gave some to her husband, who was with her, and he ate it." Adam and Eve saw something prohibited, salivated for it, then engaged in disobedience, which has caused humanity to suffer. God showcased His mercy, giving a stark warning to their sons in Genesis 4:7: "If you do what is right, won't you be accepted? But if you do not do what is right, sin is crouching at the door. Its desire is for you, but you must rule over it."

Move past seeing, exclusively, with emotions and let Godly parameters guide what you pursue. In 1 Corinthians 2:9, Paul encourages with "No eye has seen, no ear has heard, and no human heart has conceived what God has prepared for those who love him."

Little thought: Repeatedly succumbing to an unhealthy appetite is not an eye issue but a heart issue. God can change your appetite.

Operation S

In a stereotypical spy movie, someone is given a sealed manila envelope. This envelope typically contains instructions regarding a time-sensitive, covert operation and snapshots of persons of interest with the caveat "If you choose to accept this mission." This is a parallel scenario of the 2019 film *Gemini Man*. The unconventional plot unfolded with a person of interest the main character was tasked to eliminate. In this science-fiction thriller, the older man was being hunted by his younger clone assassin. The main character had to fight with himself figuratively and literally for freedom. He could not rely on his own strengths, strategies, and intellect because he was fighting his clone. He needed resources and tactics outside of himself to overcome his foe.

Self-reflection is the daunting process all must endure if there is a desire to achieve a better version of oneself. This process of self-awareness allows an honest evaluation of intent and actions. If we choose to accept this overt operation on Self, we will be plucked from the center of our universe and experience the freedom of emotional and spiritual maturity that God desires. It says in Jeremiah 9:23–24a, "The wise person should not boast in his wisdom; the strong should not boast in his strength; the wealthy should not boast in his wealth. But the one who boasts should boast in this: that he understands and knows me."

Little thought: Only truth can buttress who you are and who you were made to be.

Remember Me

As you mind your business in a market or perhaps at a gas station, on occasion a person from your past will initiate those famous words of entrapment: "Remember me?" A fog and a blank stare overtake you as you feverishly comb through mental records, only to garner the awkward response of "No."

It is natural and appropriate to ask, "Where is God?" in times of misfortune, even to wonder if He is listening to constant pleas for providence. This mirrors the plight of the book of Habakkuk. This book is littered with the questions of why hard times came and how long will they last. In times of loneliness, deflation, and regret, there is an innate yearning to feel safe and affirmed. A loose paraphrase of the prophet's conclusion in chapter 3 verse 18 is, although things have been bad, and have become worse, and still have a more dreadful potential; "Yet I will rejoice in the LORD, I will be joyful in God my Savior."

We can echo these sentiments because, even in the silence, the reputation of God can be trusted.

Little thought: Remembering God is important, but true solace is found when embracing the promise that He remembers us.

Chemical Reaction

One day, when my oldest daughter was five years old, she was helping me clean the dishes. We were having a conversation about a liquid that spilled, and like an unexpected roar of thunder, she exclaimed, "Daddy, maybe it was a non-Newtonian fluid!"

Resembling a good father, I played along and cautiously affirmed her assessment while using the nearest smartphone to covertly learn about this mysterious fluid. A summary of this fluid is that it responds, on a molecular level, to the pressure applied to it. Simply put, if you hit this fluid with enough force, the molecules harden, resulting in the fluid becoming stiff. However, if you gently stir the fluid, the molecules are unresponsive, resulting in a watery form.

If you have lived longer than five years, you will quickly discover life consists of trouble. Trouble is guaranteed, but peace is an internal resolution despite external pressure.

At the onset of being crucified, Jesus spoke not as a victim but a victor, saying in John 16:33, "I have told you these things so that in me you may have peace. You will have suffering in this world. Be courageous! I have conquered the world." Our human construct is to push against anything uncomfortable, but the ebbs and flows of life require more fluidity. There's never a guarantee that a situation will change for the better; however, even when a situation fails to change, we can be changed while in the situation.

Little thought: Jesus offers peace even in peril.

No Time for Noise

The human body is an awe-inspiring machine; there are many things that occur within our bodies voluntarily and involuntarily. Tunnel vision is, oftentimes, one of those involuntary phenomena that happen when under extreme stress but can be managed. There is another form of tunnel vision that affects the hearing called *auditory exclusion*. While a mother is giving birth, a TV could be on, but she can't hear it because her mind is telling her ears that it's not important. Or when husbands, watching a ballgame have the superpower of tuning out task details due to this auditory wonder. Whether it's voluntary or involuntary, this practice is the brain informing the body there is no time for unnecessary noise.

Prior to the book of Nehemiah, the nation of Israel had been overtaken by Persia (modern-day Iran), and its people had become prisoners of war. In Nehemiah's adult life, a homeland return of some Jewish natives had been approved. (See Nehemiah 1:3–4, 2:5–6). A theme strewn throughout the previous book of Ezra and this book is rebuilding while facing opposition. Nehemiah's task was to rebuild Jerusalem's walls; however, if anyone had just cause to do nothing, it would have been him. He was in a position of prominence as the king's cupbearer (translation: he had a cushy job), and the wall that he was attempting to rebuild had been destroyed for seventy-plus years (translation: no one was a successful builder prior to him). He was moved with emotion but was led by prayer. Nehemiah 6:3–4 reports, "I sent messengers to them, saying, 'I am doing important work and cannot come down. Why should the work cease while I leave it and go down to you?' Four times they sent me the same proposal, and I gave them the same reply."

While he was working on the wall, there was not simply the noise of construction but also that of conflict. On five separate occasions, he faced opposition, but Nehemiah's focus was not on what others said and not even on what he thought of his own ability but on his God-given purpose. Sometimes the loudest noise we must silence comes from within. Don't believe me? Consider Jesus. In a garden, while under the stress of his impending execution, he asked the Father in Luke 22:42, "Father, if you are willing, take this cup [task] away from me," but He refocused on His purpose and refused to concede.

Little thought: Do not let internal and external voices define you. Allow your Creator to define you.

Misdirected Energy

Throughout history, monarchs have often been charged to be more than simply the regal symbol of a nation. In times of turmoil, they must be chief strategist in a variety of initiatives, be they economic, political, or military. In the recount of Joshua, Israel had no king but relied on God Almighty to be the chief strategist and conqueror, while Joshua was the human representative chosen to lead this nation. When faced with the enemy nation of Ai, it's king exhibited a common mistake that led to his nation's downfall: misdirected energy.

Joshua 8:14 provides a summation of this military misstep.

> When the king of Ai saw
> the Israelites, the men of the city
> hurried and went out early in
> the morning so that he and all
> his people could engage Israel in
> battle at a suitable place facing

the Arabah. But he did not know
there was an ambush waiting for
him behind the city.

It was right and proper for the king of the nation to send his troops to engage the threat; however, when they passionately and completely pursued in one direction, they left the city and presumably their queen unprotected. Only one move remained for the victorious army of Israel—checkmate.

Little thought: Learning patience takes patience. Do not be mastered by anything, even your good intentions.

War

In 2014, a well-known group of toys was enshrined into the National Toy Hall of Fame. Among them were the stationary figures called little green army men. Many children have found themselves entertained with these soldiers as they engulfed themselves in imaginary epochs of war since the 1930s. A war is made of a series of battles among opposing forces. Whether it's international competition, national unrest, religious division, or familial angst, one word can easily surmise the series of internal and external conflict: *war*.

Exodus 17 presents a reintroduction of a newly liberated nation named Israel. It sought a homeland. However, during their trek, we see a three-pronged war that raged in their time and visits us today:

- The battle inside (verses 1–7) shows the internal strife.
- The battle outside (verses 8–9) exhibits the fight against outside factors.

- The unseen battle (verses 10–16) alludes to the spiritual struggle between good and evil.

The high point of the narrative is not only victory but also Moses's naming the war sight. He chose Jehovah Nissi, translated to mean "the LORD is my Banner." During their day, a banner was not merely a flag but also an intentional symbol of who you represent and what authority backs you.

This God that was embraced by Moses gives all the ability not to be stationary soldiers but victors in this war called life.

Little thought: In life's series of battles, you have an ally in God Almighty.

Baby and the Birds Have Lunch

I was enjoying lunch at an outside eatery and saw a pregnant woman shuffling her way to the pickup counter for her meal. While busy people were watching, I was ambushed by three little sparrows. They surrounded my chair and enjoyed the buffet of scraps on the ground. One was so bold as to leap on the chair across from me and simply stand there. Obviously, I wasn't looking for trouble, so I crushed a chip and offered it as a gesture of peace.

This lunchtime fiasco resonated with me because of the passage I was, coincidentally, reading. In Matthew 6, Jesus was giving a how-to seminar on prayer, giving generously, and maintaining peace. Within the portion that addressed navigating through self-induced stress, He spoke of not worrying about everyday life. Concerns over resources are valid; however, these should not supersede a trust in the Source. Despite having no money or logical means, that day, the baby and the birds had lunch. Matthew 6:25–31 instructs,

Therefore, I tell you, don't worry about your life, what you will eat or what you will drink; or about your body, what you will wear. Isn't life more than food and the body more than clothing? Consider the birds of the sky: They don't sow or reap or gather into barns, yet your heavenly Father feeds them. Aren't you worth more than they? Can any of you add one moment to his life span by worrying? And why do you worry about clothes? Observe how the wildflowers of the field grow: They don't labor or spin thread. Yet I tell you that not even Solomon in all his splendor was adorned like one of these. If that's how God clothes the grass of the field, which is here today and thrown into the furnace tomorrow, won't he do much more for you—you of little faith? So don't worry, saying, 'What will we eat?' or 'What will we drink?' or 'What will we wear?' For the Gentiles eagerly seek all these things, and your heavenly Father knows that you need them. But seek first the kingdom of God and his righteousness, and all these things will be provided for you. Therefore, don't worry about tomorrow, because tomorrow will worry about itself. Each day has enough trouble of its own.

Little thought: At times, God will provide relief. Other times, He will provide peace amidst unwelcome conditions. Whatever He provides, embrace the Provider.

Can't Stop a Blink

A man and his wife received news that they'd be having a child soon. Overjoyed, they began to prepare their home for their new arrival by child-proofing everything and buying countless stuffed animals and the softest blankies they could find. One night, the man's wife said the two whimsical words that changed their lives forever: "It's time!" They spent several hours at the hospital, and finally, they met their beautiful baby girl. The father held her in his arms and whispered to her all night, but he made one crucial mistake: he blinked.

He blinked once and saw her walking, then running everywhere. He blinked again, and she began talking and quickly talking back! Again he blinked, and she was riding the school bus. Then he blinked again, and she began driving past the school bus. Although he tried not to, he blinked once more and found himself at the doorway of a church as his baby girl stood at the footsteps of marriage.

As time passes and people change for the better or the worse, we must realize that God was, is, and will always be consistent. You may have blinked, but use what time you have and enjoy it. Now is the time because whether you like it or not, these two are true: time will not wait, and you can't stop a blink.

> Pay careful attention, then, to how you walk, not as unwise people but as wise making the most of the time. (Ephesians 5:15–16)

Little thought: As time passes, it's easier to embrace God's promises even though he does not promise explanations.

One-Way Trip

One day, a wife beamed as she opened her mailbox and paraded around the house with joy.

Naturally, her husband was curious about her excitement and asked, "What was the letter in the mail?"

She replied, "It's an invitation to Sarah's wedding!"

Puzzled and unenthused, he asked, "Who is Sarah?"

She explained that this invite came from a woman she befriended at her job a few days prior. She later asked her husband to accompany her to the event, and he reluctantly agreed.

On the day of the event, she noticed her husband's displeasure but tried to lighten the mood and enjoy the ceremony. As he daydreamed and restlessly moved in his seat, he glanced at his wife; and to his astonishment, she was blissfully gazing at the wedding party and silently mouthing every word of the wedding vows.

While traveling back home, the man exclaimed, "I don't understand how you can get so much pleasure during the wedding of a person you really don't know." In his condescension, he resolved, "I guess it's a female thing."

At this point, his wife burst into tears, expressing, "I thank you for coming with me, but you've done everything in your power to show your discontent. You even went as far as to often check your phone for the ball game updates. It's true that I'm not close to her, it is true that the ceremony was long, and it's also true that we knew absolutely no one in attendance. But the unfortunate truth about today is that you could not fully embrace the journey of where we've come because your focus was solely on where you wanted to be."

Like the husband, it is easy to be lulled by current comfort and forward focus while overlooking past development.

> So what do people get in this life for all their hard work and anxiety? Their days of labor are filled with pain and grief; even at night their minds cannot rest. It is all meaningless. So,

> I decided there is nothing better
> than to enjoy food and drink and
> to find satisfaction in work. Then
> I realized that these pleasures are
> from the hand of God. (Ecclesi-
> astes 2:22–24 NLT)

Little thought: Getting to your desired destination should never come at the cost of your reflective appreciation.

A Nuclear Misunderstanding

Since the 1960s, the president of the United States and a small number of delegates have access to the president's emergency satchel. Also known as the Football, this leather briefcase contains a system of top secret codes and initiators that provide the president the ability to begin a sequence of releasing the country's nuclear munitions. There is a myriad of reasons that so few of these beyond-exclusive personnel have access to this. Primary among these justifications is that the more people privy to this capability, the more potential for unfit emotions to fuel a *possible* global disaster.

Joshua, chapter 22, demonstrates how erratic emotions can cause a dynamic eruption that bears long-lasting impacts. There was civil war brewing among two tribes in Israel because of an assumption. The tribe of Gad perceived that a sister tribe named Manasseh turned from their God and erected an idol for worship. Although this was not the case, Verses 11–12 show that in their haste, Gad was preparing to exercise the nuclear option. A moment of sober consideration provided the clarity and communication needed to curtail the disaster. A small group of delegates traveled to their neighboring tribe and sought to resolve the discrepancy between their perception and reality. This endeavor proved to halt the potentially nuclear situation. Although this narrative conveys the lesson of "Do not assume," it also demonstrates the dangers of minimizing a misunderstanding because if things are not quickly addressed and resolved the consequences may be combustible.

Little thought: Consider tomorrow's outcomes when making today's decisions.

Where Am I in This Picture?

A common trend on social media has been flashback Fridays. This is when someone posts pictures from their past with the intent to reflect and laugh—a lot. One major resource used in flashing back is the use of school yearbooks. Upon receiving the yearbook, the immediate question to the child is, "Where are you?"

If you have ever casually read the Bible or perhaps attended a religious gathering, a similar question may arise among all the King James rhetoric: "Where am I in this picture?" A theme woven throughout Scripture is about those that belong to God. A depiction of this is culminated with the use of sheep in John 10:3–10, 3:14, which says,

> The gatekeeper opens it
> for him, and the sheep hear his
> voice. He calls his own sheep by
> name and leads them out. When
> he has brought all his own out-

side, he goes ahead of them. The sheep follow him because they know his voice. They will never follow a stranger; instead, they will run away from him, because they don't know the voice of strangers." Jesus gave them this figure of speech, but they did not understand what he was telling them. Jesus said again, "Truly I tell you; I am the gate for the sheep. All who came before me are thieves and robbers, but the sheep didn't listen to them. I am the gate. If anyone enters by me, he will be saved and will come in and go out and find pasture. A thief comes only to steal and kill and destroy. I have come so that they may have life and have it in abundance. I am the good shepherd. I know my own, and my own know me.

In the collage of life, you matter and are a unique part of history's big picture. The Master Artist isn't put off by your past but desires to use all the brush-strokes of your life to paint a picture filled with His amazing grace.

Little thought: Even when you are considered to be outside the lines, you matter in the big picture.

What's in Your Hands?

One of the most unsettling moments as a caretaker is having a toddler who can barely communicate show a guilty demeanor, with their hands behind their back. The natural and abrupt question is usually "What's in your hands?" This sometimes results in an admission of guilt, but more often than not, the standard answer is "Nothing." Although this is an elementary parody of life with a child, the principal of this question is a biblical one.

When Moses and the nation of Israel stood at the bank of the Red Sea, God made a simple inference: "Use what's in your hand."

> The Lord said to Moses, "Why are you crying out to me? Tell the Israelites to break camp. As for you, lift your staff, stretch out your hand over the sea, and divide it so that the Israelites can go through the sea on dry

ground. Then Moses stretched out his hand over the sea. The Lord drove the sea back with a powerful east wind all that night and turned the sea into dry land. So, the waters were divided. Then the Lord said to Moses, "Stretch out your hand over the sea so that the water may come back on the Egyptians, on their chariots and horsemen." So, Moses stretched out his hand over the sea, and at daybreak the sea returned to its normal depth. While the Egyptians were trying to escape from it, the Lord threw them into the sea. (Exodus 14:15–16, 14:21, 14:26–27)

Moses had a habit we all share: making excuses. However, progress in life requires less excuses and more adjustments. With proper perspective, opposition can be opportunity. All Moses had was a walking stick, and that was enough because God didn't need anything except obedience.

Little thought: God is not primarily interested in calling those that are equipped. He has a history of equipping those He calls.

Happily *Even* After

A couple was attending a gala celebrating their wedding anniversary. This couple had immense love for each other but a peculiar sense of humor. Once the gifts were presented and kind regards shared, the husband took center stage to bring a conclusion to this grand event. He reflected on their nuptials and expressed, "It is nothing short of an honor and a privilege for this woman to be married to me! She has been by my side through my health issues, with me during my money issues, and is the main cause of my mental issues."

After the husband finished his "heartfelt" sentiments, everyone focused on the wife and demanded a rebuttal.

The elderly woman rose to her feet and said smugly, "I love you too, but I had it worse."

With a smile, her husband asked, "How so, dear?"

She eloquently exclaimed, "Sure, you've been married to me, but you've never had the misfortune of being married to you!"

Although this couple meant no malice, some of life's interactions are saturated with genuine animosity. Many family trees are littered with nuts that refuse to reconcile. As we examine the actions of others, we will encounter allegations, wrongs, and a bevy of unresolvable nuances. The possibility of intimate love presents the possibility of great hurt. Tempering expectations and extending grace leads to a life lived happily, even after adversity.

> When a person's ways please the LORD he makes even his enemies to be at peace with him. Better a little with righteousness than great income with injustice. (Proverbs 16:7–8)

Little thought: How are you prepared to live today if you never receive what you are owed from yesterday?

Thirsty for a Cure

When we or our loved ones are sick for a lengthy period, we seek sage advice from the international physician named Google. We input our symptoms and scroll a myriad of possibilities. While doing so, we have the propensity to resonate with the worst possible outcomes. A cough must be an upper respiratory infection, and a slight irritation is undoubtedly a bite from a spider indigenous to a Brazilian rainforest. As the world grew weary during the COVID-19 crisis of 2020, the Groundhog Day news cycle presented a constant barrage of increased fatalities and recommended mitigation measures. The world grew thirsty for a cure. With a cursory glance at human history—whether the problem is an international health crisis, socioeconomic instabilities, or the rotten apples on our family tree—we see humanity's thirst for a cure.

When one is faced with a deathly ailment, the word *cure* is the best news; however, the best alternative is the word *remission*. *Remission* simply means either the reduction or recession of a disease. Although we will not be able to escape the presence of sin, the impact of its allure can be in a state of remission. When Jesus sacrificed Himself on the cross, He presented humanity with the cure for the penalty of sin while simultaneously presenting a means for grace while living in our fallen world. First John 2:1–2 encourages, "My little children, I am writing you these things so that you may not sin. But if anyone does sin, we have an advocate with the Father; Jesus Christ the righteous one. He himself is the atoning sacrifice for our sins, and not only for ours, but also for those of the whole world."

Little thought: Identify the condition, seek proper counsel, and walk toward the cure.

Proper Perspective

An anxious college freshman wrote a letter to his parents reading, "As you may or may not know, my dormitory burned down, but I really don't think it had anything to do with the narcotics my roommates and I were enjoying. You always taught me, 'Safety first!' I'm looking forward to the weekend. That's when my new girlfriend Lady Smoke and I are getting married, because she's pregnant. You always taught me that having a family matters! Well, in honesty, the dorm didn't burn down, I wouldn't know what to do with drugs, and lastly, I've never met a Lady named Smoke. However, the truth is I'm flunking physics."

This clever young man forced his parents to view the present challenge in light of a larger perspective. By submitting to a belief in an eternal God, our lives should be lived with eternity in mind. This simply means looking past your current state and viewing the totality of life from a bird's-eye view. This does not negate fear, nor does it deflect adverse circumstances. However, it gives the present pain a purpose.

The human heart naturally pursues what it values. Proper perspective is leaning the heart's pursuits in the right direction.

> Let your eyes look forward; fix your gaze straight ahead. Carefully consider the path for your feet, and all your ways will be established. (Proverbs 4:25–26)

Little thought: Perspective is not what you see but how you see what you see.

Bubbles

I can vividly recall sitting in the grass with my daughters, enjoying the wistful breeze of autumn air, the clear sky, and a new bottle of bubbles. We enjoyed the whimsical dance of each bubble as we gently blew through the wand and watched, amazed at both the big and the small ones that immediately popped. It was easy to ignore outside distractions while submerging myself in this moment with my princesses. Occasionally, I would remind them that although the bubbles were inviting, they should be cautious because if they popped in their eyes, it would be harmful.

The year 2020 was considered to be a pivotal moment in history, with the frequency of international sociopolitical unrest, and the minor issue of a global pandemic. New words and phrases became ingrained in societal vernacular, such as *social distancing, new normal,* and let's not forget that the interchangeable use of the words *quarantine* and *bubble.*

In Luke 9:32–33, Jesus taught Peter and the rest of His students to resist the bubble.

> Peter and those with him were in a deep sleep, and when they became fully awake, they saw his glory and the two men who were standing with him. As the two men were departing from him, Peter said to Jesus, "Master, it's good for us to be here. Let's set up three shelters: one for you, one for Moses, and one for Elijah" not knowing what he was saying.

In Jesus's day, biblical text primarily consisted of two sections: the law and the prophets. The main question regarding Jesus during His day has recurred throughout history: "Was He who He claimed to be?" This passage is primarily about the confirmation of Jesus's identity as fully God and fully man, but there is an additional underlying tension.

Peter offered an unsolicited idea in verse 33 to create three memorials to show honor to three great leaders, but he was ignored. Why was he ignored?

There are at least two problems with Peter's proposal. Building three memorials implies that Moses, Elijah, and Jesus were equals and the second issue brings us back to bubbles. Peter's statement infers that they should remain in private worship and forgo Jesus's public work.

It was undoubtedly good for them to privately be with Jesus, but there was still work to be done. This passage purposefully concludes in verse 37 with "The next day, when they came down from the mountain, a large crowd met him." Jesus was relaying to His disciples, the early church, and us today to resist the isolation of a bubble because there is much work to do. Resisting the bubble requires walking toward the broken and caring for the unloved.

Little thought: In a world of tribalism and cyber isolation, we must resist bubbles.

Slaughterhouse

While I wholeheartedly endorse a healthy life-style, I occasionally enjoy my share of salty, chocolaty, or fried goodness. However, I would rather not see the process it takes to get meats from the stable to the table. It's a messy task to kill, gut, and clean an animal. Consider your local butcher, who is most of the time dressed in white, coming out the back of the meat section, with bloodstains and severed skin all over their apron and boots.

Many ceremonial sacrifices were for the Jewish culture of the day, they were done for various reasons. When God taught His people to worship Him, He put great emphasis on sacrifices. Why? Animal sacrifices accomplished at least two purposes: (1) the animal symbolically took the sinners' place and paid the penalty for them by death, and (2) the animal's death represented one life given so another can be saved and forgiven. Simply put, to satisfy this holy God, there needed to be a penalty paid by which forgiveness could be granted.

The animal was not a main course fried to perfection, nor was it an entrée garnished with veggies and dashed with pepper. It was a substitute. Over time this process turned the nation of Israel into a messy slaughterhouse with blood, guts, and unrepentant people everywhere. God saw that with so much sin, a more powerful substitute would be needed as penance.

> Under the old system, the blood of goats and bulls and the ashes of a young cow could cleanse people's bodies from ceremonial impurity. Just think how much more the blood of Christ will purify our consciences from sinful deeds so that we can worship the living God. For by the power of the eternal Spirit, Christ offered himself to God as a perfect sacrifice for our sins. (Hebrews 9:13–14 NLT)

Little thought: There can be beautiful outcomes after the messy work of forgiveness.

Remember for a Purpose

The evidence of getting older is shown in many ways. Randomly we experience body aches, and for some, hair begins to thin or gray exceptionally early. But one of the most common indicators is forgetting things such as phones, keys, or even a wallet. An excellent method to stave off this annoyance is to have an established home for each item. This, of course, builds repetition. Even from infancy, we learn and retain information by the repetition of phrases and tasks.

Typology is an elaborate way of saying "the examination of repeated phrases or themes to better understand the whole story." Throughout the Bible, there is a repeated theme of remembering. The importance of this repeated advisory can be deduced to the little phrase of "remember for a purpose." Remember the failures to counsel others, remember pain to properly process, and remember certain events to celebrate.

Psalm 90:12 says, "Teach us to number our days carefully so that we may develop wisdom in our hearts."

Embedded in us is the inclination to focus on what's next, but we benefit from tempering our ambition with appreciation of our journey and considering the lessons along the way. Never settle for constantly moving ahead, but aspire to remember for a purpose.

Little thought: Healthy reflection equips you to refocus and reengage.

Empty House on Memory Lane

Aboy was coming of age in a house that held many expectations and experiences. As he built a life for himself, he chose to move away and commit to hard work and career progression. As the years passed, the house that held his memories stood dilapidated and for sale. With the financial fruits of his labor, he quickly purchased the house. Enduring a magnetic pull, he found himself frequently stopping by and simply staring. He dared never to step inside, sell it, or demolish it. It was as if the structure mirrored its new owner in being stuck in time. No one knew if this man was reliving a house of horrors or if his memories were of long-passed love.

A foundation of emotional stability is to stand at the entrance of memory lane, visiting every house and accepting that not everything was your fault and that you can't fix everything. Process and address those things within your power and attempt to reconcile with the rest.

Although our past may have calloused us to mistrust a person or even an institution, the character of God is trustworthy.

> "When I am afraid, I will
> trust in you. (Psalm 56:3)

Little thought: Never let *could've*, *would've*, and *should've* magnify yesterday, hinder today, or paint tomorrow the shade of worry.

Strength in Gentleness

Every Christmas, I get the privilege of being asked by my bride what I'd like for dinner. And almost every Christmas, I request her renowned lasagna. One Christmas, I was in full "Garfield the cat" mode and refused to wait for our guests. In my haste, I grabbed an elegant china dish and gave my lasagna slice a wonderful home. Conversely, she was sensible and waited to use a disposable plate. Which plate held the food better? The truth is, because we didn't have flimsy plastic plates, both dishes held the food adequately. With one, you can handle with less care because it was made to be temporary. The other is delicate and was crafted to be treated with caution and gentleness.

Gentleness is not the opposite of strength but a sober and controlled application of strength. The Bible is filled with passages on sobriety, but the majority of these references refer to being sober minded. Biblical sobriety is wide-ranging and refers to anything that inhibits your ability to make a rationalized and righteous decision. When the nuances of personal and professional life call for blind emotions, call on the strength of gentleness. Philippians 4:5–7 cautions, "Let your graciousness be known to everyone. The Lord is near. Don't worry about anything, but in everything, through prayer and petition with thanksgiving, present your requests to God. And the peace of God, which surpasses all understanding, will guard your hearts and minds in Christ Jesus."

Little thought: Sometimes your greatest strength is exercising self-control.

Good News in a Bad Time

B en and Joe had been convicted and sentenced to prison for two unrelated cases of armed robbery. As time passed, these cellmates began to discover more about each other, including being from the same neighborhood, sharing similar hobbies, and even a fond humor about being convicted of the same crime.

Ben told Joe, "You're my buddy. I'll never leave you."

Likewise, Joe conveyed to Ben, "You're my main man. I wouldn't think to leave you either."

At the next moment, the corrections officer came to Ben and said, "You've just made parole."

In an instant, the forever-friendship rhetoric shifted to Ben telling Joe, "I've got to go."

Ben received good news in a bad time.

The narrative in Joshua 1:1–7 is about the death of Moses and the transition of Joshua to the leadership position. We read of a nation of over 1 million people asking the same question: "Now what?"

The seismic loss of Moses cast a cloud over an entire nation. God acknowledged this unforgiving reality: Moses was dead.

Life is not about choosing faith or reality but faith despite reality. Change is unavoidable; however, progress hinges on the adjustments made during the now-what moments.

Mark 16:9–15 shares a similar account of a major loss and a now-what moment. Jesus's disciples received the good news that their teacher was the risen Savior yet continued to weep in disbelief. As they reclined at the table, pondering the now-what, they soon discovered their forever friend would deliver the Good news despite their bad times.

Little thought: Even during bad times, God has a plan.

Beauty in the Untweetable

In many spectrums of twenty-first-century advertisement, the apex of online circulation is to go viral. For better or worse, this has been the goal for many, including some churches. In 2013, a pastor of a church in Canton, Ohio, felt the story of Easter needed some sprucing up. The narrative that includes an innocent man being killed and a miraculous resurrection apparently needed pyrotechnics. Insert indoor fireworks at an annual church play. The actor portraying Jesus was supposed to kick out of the tomb with an array of controlled explosives going off as he raised his fist in victorious Rocky Balboa fashion. When the fireworks went off, the tomb caught fire, and "Jesus" was stuck inside. Mission accomplished—an unforgettable Easter Sunday.

This event, unfortunately, typifies the religious car salesman's approach: promises of features and gimmicks to attract passersby for an experience that will benefit them today but do little to sustain them tomorrow. God's Word and His promises are enough.

First Thessalonians 4:11 admonishes, "Make it your goal to live a quiet life, minding your own business and working with your hands, just as we instructed you before. Then people who are not believers will respect the way you live, and you will not need to depend on others."

Little thought: Strive for a maturing life and be okay if it does not go viral.

What Are You Looking At?

Whatever demographic you find yourself in, there are words and phrases that can stir emotions and undoubtedly arrest your attention. One such phrase is the question "What are you looking at?" With perceived aggression, this simple question has caused communal conflict to crescendo into an unhinged brawl. It has even aroused an argument or two among spouses as a wife addresses her husband's alleged wandering eye.

In Isaiah 6:1–5, the prophet describes a vision conveying the gravitas of God's glory. The beginning of his account recalls, "In the year that King Uzziah died, I saw the Lord seated on a high and lofty throne, and the hem of his robe filled the temple." There are at least two reasons this passage starts with documenting the year. The first is to chronicle the date of the vision. The second reason is to remind the original audience of that year's importance.

King Uzziah had one of the most prosperous reigns in Israel's history. Under his rule, the northern

Israeli kingdom experienced military and economic success. In fact, archeology credits him as an early developer of the current-day catapult (2 Chronicles 26:15). For fifty-two years, this monarch reigned, and the nation experienced success. But when his pride resulted in his eventual death, there was nothing short of uncertainty in the land (2 Chronicles 26). What would happen to the military and the economy? What would happen to all the comforts the citizens enjoyed? Among all these realities, Isaiah pronounced, "I saw the Lord."

John 12:40–41 refers to this passage and reveals that the one on the throne was the glorified Jesus. His throne being high and lofty signified His celestial position; however, the edge of His robe filling the temple refers to His nearness. With all the supernatural things that crossed Isaiah's line of sight, there was an intentional focus on the God that saves.

Little thought: When we see God accurately, we see the world, our situations, and ourselves more accurately.

A Better Yes

Traditionally, children are raised to identify right from wrong to equip for adulthood. Then as an adult, with this upbringing, it is often easier to differentiate right from wrong; however, the struggle now is to discern right from almost right. Our day is one where truth is relative and opinions are in a container labeled Flavor of the Month. With the whirlwind of self-centered ideologies, it is natural to often be in search of something better.

In a garden named Eden, God relayed to Adam and Eve all approved things that they should say yes to. Such as in our current day, they were deceived in believing there was a better yes. This pride was the practice that poisoned their paradise. This deception led to actions that conveyed a belief that there was an acceptable alternative to God's instructions. To be sure, there is never an acceptable alternative to what God says on a matter: "For every one of God's promises is 'Yes' in Him [Jesus]. Therefore, through him we also say 'Amen' to the glory of God" (2 Corinthians 1:20).

Little thought: Be careful in searching for a better yes when God has spoken. Your Father has the best yes.

Expectations

Before becoming calloused by life's disappointments, children have an innocent and unwavering faith. They ask and expect to receive every request. Logistics and finances are mere molehills at the feet of their wildest dreams. Although life may alter the level of our expectations, we should never stop desiring the right kinds of things. As children, we ask our parents for toys and every other shiny gadget; as teens, we ask to be left alone because we know everything; and as adults, we ask for promotions, tax exemptions, and more shiny gadgets.

Although expectancy is natural, unfortunately, so are unmet expectations. We should be aware of realities and their implications; but like children, we should have unwavering faith that all things have the potential to be for God's glory, our good, and someone else's betterment.

Romans 8:28–29 pronounces, "We know that all things work together for the good of those who love God, who are called according to his purpose.

For those he foreknew he also predestined to be conformed to the image of his Son, so that he would be the firstborn among many brothers and sisters."

Little thought: What childlike attributes should you revive?

Think Again

Most outdoor games with children are fun, even as an adult, assuming you have the time and the energy to play. Freeze tag remains at the top of my list. Someone runs or hides, but if they are tagged, they are unable to move (hence, frozen) until a teammate can unfreeze them. Frequently giving my children an advantage, I would stand still until they are charging toward me; and at the last possible minute, I would emphatically dodge them while screaming, "Think again!" This often resulted in me being frozen anyway, but it is always enjoyable times.

As we regularly interact with others, our intentions are rarely the problem. The chief culprit that causes contention to smolder is how we carry out our intentions. When someone is cooking, their intent is to create not only a filling meal but also one that is flavorful. Just as one precisely prepares and seasons a meal, likewise, we should take caution of our words and actions. This is the important incremental work of the Holy Spirit.

Colossians 4:5–6 expresses, "Act wisely toward outsiders, making the most of the time. Let your speech always be gracious, seasoned with salt, so that you may know how you should answer each person."

Little thought: When concerns become constant worries, resolve to think again.

On Your Mark

For a few hundred years, the Olympic Games have taken place, and for many the highlight has been the track-and-field events. Every athlete's preparation is done with gold in mind. Their focus forces their actions to mirror their aspirations. After finally qualifying, the competitors are tasked to exceed expectations and endure to victory.

The journey of life is often viewed as a race, not that its participants should jostle for position but one that has varying obstacles and requirements of endurance. An enduring principle of a progressive life is to walk toward incremental goals with patient ambition.

A coach will reprimand repeated errors and push their competitor to a point of exhaustion, but these measures are done with victory in mind. The same can be said of the ever-present celestial coach. He desires life's participants to experience victory,

even in moments of defeat. He is not a silent specta-
tor but an active help throughout this marathon.

> Let us lay aside every hin-
> drance and the sin that so eas-
> ily ensnares us. Let us run with
> endurance the race that lies before
> us, keeping our eyes on Jesus, the
> pioneer and perfecter of our faith.
> For the joy that lay before him,
> he endured the cross, despising
> the shame, and sat down at the
> right hand of the throne of God.
> (Hebrews 12:1–2)

Little thought: In the monotony and missteps of life,
this race is winnable by God's grace.

Broken

A master potter gained his reputation by producing the finest and most unique pieces of pottery. He crafted a small decorative piece adorned with diamonds, rubies, and other exotic accents; but, shockingly, over a lengthy period, this piece began to crack. Over time, the pottery changed ownership several times. As it was in another's possession, the new owner tried to address the discrepancies by inputting more fixtures to imitate the vessel's original glory. Ultimately, only the master potter could repair the vessel because he knew the original image and remembered the purposeful position of each jewel.

Humanity reflects this broken vessel. Sculpted by heavenly hands, mankind was made perfect; however, through the injection of sin, every generation has had a marred reality. This downward trend has equated to the degradation of the beautiful creation we were made to be.

These barriers of brokenness, if addressed, can become the very means that bring closeness to the creator. In the mental health profession, addressing emotional brokenness means to identify, explore, and resolve. This process can be summarized as recognizing the trauma or existing malady with the expectation of eventually restoring emotional stability.

As a potter cannot fully restore a piece until it is broken, our creator cannot fully restore us unless we are willing to be broken. Full restoration is only attainable by the one who knows you best: the Master Potter.

> You do not want a sacrifice, or I would give it; you are not pleased with a burnt offering. The sacrifice pleasing to God is a broken spirit. You will not despise a broken and humbled heart, God. (Psalm 51:16–17)

Little thought: Brokenness is not a conclusion; it's the best posture for repair.

Conditions of Unconditional Love

Two events that can cause a family immense joy or colossal chaos are funerals and weddings. These occurrences tend to convey the display or loss of love. Depending on your cultural background, some weddings consist of the groom walking down the aisle with his party, with each sides the aisle filled with people to witness an exchange of promises. After the groom takes his place, the bride walks down the same aisle, concluding with the covenantal promise of commitment and ending with a loving kiss.

Today, if we wanted to have a legally binding document between two parties, we would draft a contract, but in ancient times, a more common term was *covenant*. In Genesis 15:6–10, 15:17–18, God chose to show Abraham His love by making a covenant with him.

In this culture, a contract/covenant would consist of two parties bringing certain animals together and cutting them in half. After the halves were laid on separate sides, the participants would walk between the blood-soaked ground. All this symbolism was to convey the idea that if one side violated the contract/covenant, they agreed to pay with their life.

God used this bizarre vision to clarify the participants of this covenant. The vision does not show Abraham as a participant of this contract; he is simply the recipient. In essence, God was walking through the halves with Himself, showing Abraham that there was a condition to His unconditional love, and that condition was acceptance.

This strange story revolves around faithfulness. God keeping His promises hinged on faithfulness. Fortunately for Abraham and us, the faithfulness that lies in question is not of our own but of God. God's love was on full display, showing that He alone could meet the faithfulness required for His unconditional love.

Little thought: The conditions of God's unconditional love are His faithfulness and our acceptance.

Fishing Miracle

The Bible's literary composition often presents the reality of the supernatural by first teaching about the simplicity of the natural. The master teacher, Jesus, often used this in His teaching style. This same God-man that performed miracles also enjoyed a good meal and a nap. After His confirmed death, He appeared to once again be alive and enjoying time on a beach. After fishing all night, Peter and a few others caught nothing. These experienced and exhausted fishermen saw a man having breakfast ashore who suggested they cast their nets on the right side of their boat. After this seemingly pointless adjustment, they caught roughly 153 fish in an instant.

After their catch, when they went ashore, they realized this anonymous man was Jesus. After all the commotion, Jesus asked His students to join Him for breakfast on the beach. One minor detail that resonates is that they had this major haul of fish, but the overwhelming weight did not tear the net. These were poor ordinary men, with ordinary and unreliable equipment, yet the net didn't tear. At times, life releases what seems like the weight of the world, but God can keep us from falling apart. Philippians 4:19 (NLT) advises, "And this same God who takes care of me will supply all your needs from his glorious riches, which have been given to us in Christ Jesus."

Little thoughts: In life's big events, recognize the little miracles.

Ticktock

The twenty-first century can also be referred to as the hypersonic technological age, where software is hard to comprehend, hardware is antiquated upon creation, and applications are as addictive as they are helpful. Many mainstay phrases have been repurposed within this generation. A tweet is not only what a bird does but also what one's fingers can post; looking at a text is primarily done through viewing a screen than looking at a book; and *ticktock* is not relegated to a clock but, rather, the creativity of a thirty-second video upload.

For a portion of this technologically savvy generation, identity and self-worth are contingent on the number of "friends" or followers they have. For better and worse, mass media gives people a reach they would probably not have otherwise. It instantaneously allows us to be whatever version of ourselves we conjure. One ongoing battle is tempering the urge to think, *All our opinions, musings, and experiences are GOAT material.* Romans 12:3 advises us not to think too highly of ourselves, even when we're right. The aforementioned passage warns, "For by the grace given to me, I tell everyone among you not to think of himself more highly than he should think. Instead, think sensibly, as God has distributed a measure of faith to each one."

Little thought: In the rigorous pace of everyday life, how can you better slow down?

Who Are You Talking To?

Like most testosterone-filled men, I occasionally enjoy an action-filled karate film. During one film, I made haste to get back to the senseless violence, and to my surprise there was a moment of wisdom. The backdrop of the movie portrayed every character wanting to kill the main character by any means. Even with all that happening, he said, "I do not fear having crazy and foolish enemies. My fear is having crazy and foolish friends." This statement should prompt us to evaluate our friends and those we seek counsel from.

> With their words, the godless destroy their friends, but knowledge will rescue the righteous. Without wise leadership, a nation falls; there is safety in having many advisers. (Proverbs 11:9, 14 NLT)

Little thought: Inventory who and what gets the bulk of your time and consider the effects.

Counterfeit

In the final semester of undergraduate university studies, students are tasked with their final coursework, called a capstone. Mine was about the yawn-inducing topic of counterfeit currency during the Civil War. The highlight was, the more counterfeits in circulation, the more difficult it was to identify authorized currency. A major development that assisted in curtailing the circulation of counterfeits was not to master identifying the replicas but to become so familiar with the original that recognizing a counterfeit would be elementary.

The same should be said about our strengths. It is commonplace to fall in one of two categories. On one side, we can have an inflated and unrealistic view of our strengths; however, on the other side, we can grossly underappreciate our abilities. Both views are counterfeit perspectives.

Mark 12 records an interaction that saw Jesus being asked about taxes. He asked for the currency of the day, a denarius coin. He asked about the image on the coin. The crowd responded that Caesar's image was on the coin. Jesus proceeded to instruct, "Give to Cesar what is his, and give to God what is His." The implication to them and us is to consider whose image we bear. You are valuable.

Little thought: You are a unique and capable person that was made in God's image. Any other view on your identity is counterfeit.

Time Manager

B ased on millennia of data and thousands of years of research, it has been established that death has a 100 percent success rate. No matter what gender, socioeconomic status, or nationality, everyone eventually encounters and loses to the great equalizer, death. There is, conversely, the reality of embracing life within your years and not simply having years to your life. Awareness and implementation of time management will determine the trajectory of your tomorrow.

If you're experiencing constant failure in the big things, examine your management of the little things. Evaluating the small details always reveals what adjustments are needed for long-term success.

We are enthused and even enticed by someone or something that exhibits perceived perfection. The goal should be excellence, not perfection. Excellence is a pursuit to excel the best you can with the available resources. Proverbs 16:2–3, shares, "All a person's ways seem right to him, but the Lord weighs motives.

Commit your activities to the Lord, and your plans will be established." Simply put, God will take care of the *cons* if you're *pro*active about His will.

Little thought: Take time to walk with an undivided heart, an unshakeable mind, and an unparalleled passion.

Cutting the Middleman

At some point, you may have needed to troubleshoot a matter that required help-desk support. Whether it's technology, appliance malfunctions, or simply user limitation, calling someone to facilitate support and render a resolution is never a calming endeavor because it's rarely quick or easy. You may reach the general-help division, then be directed to the technical division, only for them to place you on Call Waiting to restart this quadratic equation. Redirections and intermediaries often hinder direct progress and long-term resolution.

Intimate friends have more than surface-level interaction because there is no middle man minutiae. The cover-to-cover summary of the Bible is the transition from relationship to rift and a journey back to a relationship. Jesus's direct offer of support can be found in Matthew 11:28: "Come to me, all of you who are weary and burdened, and I will give you rest."

Little thought: Relationships are difficult, but the right ones are worth the work.

All New Things or All Things New

In a bygone era, a sign of hypermasculine success was having a mirrorlike pair of dress shoes. These shoes would maintain their luster, but even with care, they would eventually require a sole replacement. For this, it was commonplace to visit a local cobbler for repairs. A cobbler is a footwear expert in taking a worn foot product and making them like new. The process does not involve giving the customer a new pair of shoes but returning the old pair of shoes restored with new life.

In Revelation, there are constant referrals to the first book, Genesis. One of the motives for this is to illustrate how God wastes nothing. With our choices made from a mind of ignorance or even a heart of rebellion, God can use every outcome to accomplish His desired intent. Revelation 21 speaks of a cosmic refresh where sin, sickness, and death are no more. Verse 5 proclaims, "And He who sits on the throne said, "Behold, I am making all things new." The declaration was not that God was making new things but that He was restoring things with new life. Despite relationships or lingering toxic emotions, He can take our old selves and make us new.

Little thought: Not everything is God's will, but He can use anything as part of His plan.

Little Things

Apious man enjoyed rendering long prayers before holiday meals. Oftentimes, by the end of his longwinded monologue, the food needed reheating. After a Thanksgiving dinner, he looked to his beloved for the warmth of June, but he received the winter of January. After some tense moments of cold shoulders, he asked his wife, "What is wrong?"

Instead of having a long discussion, she spoke his language of biblical rhetoric and simply said, "Luke 10."

Obviously, the good reverend wasn't expecting that kind of answer, but he rushed to his office to examine the reference. The chapter refers to the notable story dubbed the Good Samaritan. Verses 30 to 37 speak about the importance of love in action. One of the most revered positions of the day was that of a priest, but as he encountered a man that was beaten and robbed, he went as far as to walk past him on the opposite side of the road. Then later a man from the respected tribe of Levi failed to take pity on the same victim. Instead, it was a person without a prestigious title and devoid of cultural affluence that acted. It should be considered that these men could have justified their actions with the Law of Moses, which prohibited the handling of an unclean body; however, Jesus wanted His followers to know that doing God's will is about showing love in the little things. This pious husband was so focused on being a ministering pastor that he neglected to be a tender husband. God's will is packed with simply doing the little things that positively affects our environment.

Little thought: Don't be too busy doing God's work that you neglect to do God's will.